Wallace Milroy's

MALT WHISKY ALMANAC

A TASTER'S GUIDE

LOCHAR PUBLISHING MOFFAT · SCOTLAND

British Library Cataloguing in Publication Data

Milroy, Wallace, 1932-
  Wallace Milroy's malt whisky almanac.
  3rd ed.
  1. Scotch Whiskies
  I. Title
641.2'52

ISBN 0-948403-12-8

© Lochar Publishing 1986, 1987, 1989
Nos 7/8 The Holm
MOFFAT
DG10 9JU
Scotland
Tel: 0683-20916
Fax: 0683-21183

First edition published July 1986.
Second edition published June 1987.
Reprinted August 1987, January 1988,
October 1988.
Third edition published September 1989
Edited by Neil Wilson
Designed by Grub Street Design, London
Drawings on pages 22, 87, 90 by William
McClymont
Maps by David Langworth
Originated, printed and bound in Hong
Kong by Regent Publishing Services Ltd

Lochar Publishing gratefully acknowledges
the assistance of the Keepers of The Quaich
in the production of this work.

CONTENTS

ACKNOWLEDGEMENTS

Special thanks in the production of this book are due to:
Gordon McIntosh, Secretary to The Keepers of the
Quaich; Billy MacNeill and Roy Macmillan of United
Distillers; Colin Liddell of Guinness plc; Ross Gunn,
Douglas Shaw and Mark Lawson of Seagram Distillers;
David Urquhart of Gordon & MacPhail Ltd; Andy
Barclay of George Ballantine & Son Ltd; Moyra Peffer of
Whyte & Mackay Distillers Ltd; Hedley Wright of J&A
Mitchell & Co Ltd; Iain Doctor of Long John Distillers
Ltd; Mr IM Phillips of William Lawson Distillers Ltd;
Ron Brown of the Scotch Whisky Association; Mr A
Macfarlane and Neil Gibson of William Teacher & Sons
Ltd; Simon Richmond of Arthur Bell Distillers; Patricia
Best of Berry Bros & Rudd Ltd; Jonathan Lyddon of
Highland Distilleries Company plc; Peter JM Fairlie of
The Glenturret Distillery Ltd; John Milroy of J Milroy
Ltd; Julia Thorold of Justerini & Brooks Ltd; Decanter
Magazine; Tom Byers; Allan Hall of The Wine & Spirits
Trade Club, London; Richard O'Callaghan of Takara
Shuzo & Okura & Co Ltd; Ms Penny Weir of Wm Grant
& Sons Ltd; Ken Macrae of JR Philips Ltd; Hugh
Mitcalfe and Allan Shiach of Macallan Distillers Ltd; Tim
Hailey of Invergordon Distillers Ltd; John Grant of J&G
Grant; Jim Turle of Lang Bros Ltd; Douglas Callander of
White Heather Distillers Ltd; Sue Brown of Macdonald
& Muir Ltd; George Hocknull of Morrison Bowmore
Distillers Ltd; Irene Scott of A Bulloch & Co Ltd; Bob
Buglass of Davaar International Ltd; Tom Thomson of
United Distillers plc; Bill McCourt and Dennis Higgins of
Old Bushmills Distillery Co Ltd; Anne Dana of the
Scotch Malt Whisky Society and a special thanks to all
the distillery managers and their staff for their time,
patience and endless hospitality.

USEFUL ADDRESSES

The Scotch Whisky
Association
17 Half Moon Street
LONDON W1
Tel: 01-629-4384
Permanent displays on the
workings of a distillery with
models and Audio-Visual.
Admission free.

The Scotch Malt Whisky
Society
87 Giles Street
LEITH EH6 6BZ
Tel: 031-554-3451
Offering 10 to 20 cask
strength malts, usually
around 60% and up to 21
years old. Introductory
membership fee is £30
including a bottle of malt.

FOREWORD

In 1988 a group of leading members of the Scotch whisky industry joined forces to found an exclusive society to promote *uisge beatha* — Scotland's water of life. They named the Society *Keepers of the Quaich* to honour those around the world who recognise the nobility of Scotch whisky by working, writing and speaking on its behalf. The honour bestowed upon them is admittance to the Roll of the Keepers of the Quaich.

The symbol of the Society is a two-handled ceremonial quaich, long associated with the history of both Scotch and drinking in Scotland and which is derived from the Gaelic *cuach* — a drinking bowl. We in the industry are proud to provide the traditional contents of the quaich. The members of our Society represent the famous brand names of Scotch whisky, both the single malts and the unique delicate marriage of malt and grain whiskies known as the blends.

Wallace Milroy is not only a Keeper of the Quaich but also a renowned Scotch whisky expert and we are delighted to be associated with this, the third edition of his popular pocket book.

John AR Macphail, C.B.E.

Grand Master
Keeper of the Quaich

INTRODUCTION

It might appear ungracious of me to say that I am not surprised by the success of this book which, as I write, is entering its third edition and has sales which have surpassed 70,000 copies since publication in July 1986. But these astonishing figures are mirrored in the increasing popularity of bottled malt sales not only in the UK but also abroad. There seems to be no limit to the escalating sales graphs emanating from the export offices of those companies fortunate enough to have a malt portfolio — and yet I find myself saying "... about time too". Malt whisky is more popular now not because it has suddenly become a better product than it used to be, but simply because many whisky producers have realised that their malt portfolio is not only their most essential and precious asset, but also one of their most profitable.

Since I penned my introduction to the last edition there have been some fundamental changes in the whisky industry and in proposals for future export trading patterns. Japan's influence on exports of malt whisky from Scotland will doubtless increase as whisky is, at last, taxed on a less discriminatory basis that it has previously been. This influence has already manifested itself in the purchase of one of whisky's most evocative brand names — Ben Nevis — by one of Japan's largest whisky producers and also in the closer associations being formed between whisky producers here and large importers in Japan. If all this leads to the reopening of some of Scotland's "mothballed" distilleries then it will at first glance have been well worth the wait. If, on the other hand, it leads to a further dilution of UK ownership of malt distilleries then we may yet rue the day. However, it was the whisky barons of the last century — Dewar, Buchanan, Mackay and their ilk — who recognised the international appeal of

Scotch so perhaps it is more important not who
owns which distillery, but rather whether or not it is
producing whisky and employing people. Perhaps
my dream of seeing the resurrection of Ardbeg
Distillery — that magnificent last bastion of the
old-fashioned "big" whiskies — may yet come true.

With this new edition I am pleased to see that
once more the format and presentation have been
improved. Although all the malts are on single page
entries as before, they have been categorised by
producing region and not by *producing company.*
Thus, a malt will no longer move around the book
if it changes owner but for the aficionados who still
wish to track down the owners of each distillery,
names and addresses are given on page 140-143.
Notwithstanding that, there is a STATUS line
under each malt which does indicate the owning
company. More interestingly though I have also
indicated the age of each malt distillery so that you
can discern the "newcomers" from the more senior
drams. If you think Glenfiddich's pedigree of just
over a century is impressive then look at
Glenturret's — over 220 years!

The lists of special bottlings on pages 138 &
139 are accurate at the time of going to press. It is a
fascinating experience being confronted by the vast
selection these bottlings offer and this variety is the
second reason for the new lay-out. It is primarily
the large geographical spread of malt distilleries
throughout Scotland which manifests itself in the
product of each locality. These differences can be
detected broadly by sampling malts from a distance
apart. For example compare Bladnoch (from
Galloway), Highland Park (from Orkney),
Macallan (from Speyside) and Lagavulin (from
Islay). Try them in a blind tasting and the chances
are that even a beginner would detect the most
obvious differences. These are attributable to each
locality's distilling heritage — Lagavulin is pungent
and smokey, illustrating the distillery's use of a
peaty, soft source water and Islay's tradition of

THE MALT WHISKY PRODUCING REGIONS OF SCOTLAND AND NORTHERN IRELAND.

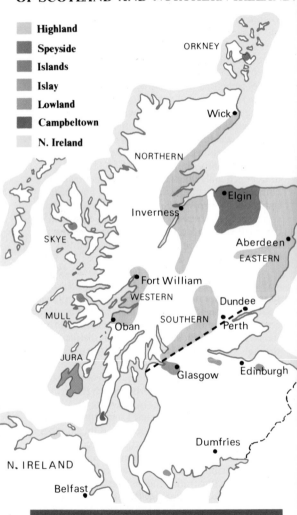

Highland
Speyside
Islands
Islay
Lowland
Campbeltown
N. Ireland

ORKNEY

Wick

NORTHERN

Elgin

Inverness

Aberdeen
EASTERN

SKYE

Fort William

WESTERN

Dundee

MULL

Oban

SOUTHERN

Perth

JURA

Glasgow

Edinburgh

Dumfries

N. IRELAND

Belfast

using peat as a fuel when drying barley. The full bodied Macallan is silky-smooth as befits a whisky matured solely in sherry casks. Bladnoch — our most southerly malt whisky distillery — is distilled on a coast caressed by the Gulf Stream where delicate, tropical plants abound. It is light, estery and fragrant — the perfect pre-dinner dram whereas at our most northerly distillery at Highland Park, the malt has a smokey flavour imbued in it from the heather-covered Orkney peat moss which is burnt in the kilns. These characteristics show that whiskies are the living embodiment of their localities and the people who make them. Your preference for each one will depend on the circumstances in which you drink it.

Within each producing region there are degrees of variation in taste, bouquet and colour which help create the hundred-plus bottled malts which are available in the UK. The alphabetical listing by region will help create not only a greater understanding of these regional variations but also of those subtle (and sometimes not so subtle) variances between malts within each region. This will all, I hope, allow you to appreciate the great depth of distilling tradition within Scotland and make your trip through the drams all the more enjoyable.

We begin on Speyside, where the greatest concentration of distilling activity in the world exists — over 50 distilleries in all. Then remaining in the Highlands we shall look at the Northern distilleries situated around Inverness and above the Moray Firth. To the East lie the distilleries nearer Banff, Aberdeen and the North Sea coast and in the Southern region of the Highlands the activity is based largely in rural Perthshire. Finally, moving over to the Western part of the Highlands, three distilleries exist in Fort William and Oban.

The Lowland region was once as busy as any other in the making of whisky, but sadly that tradition has been diminished in the last century.

However, below the imaginary line between Dundee and Greenock some nine malts are available across the whole area.

Islay produces some of the most precious and characterful malts and all eight are available from the existing distilleries on this beautiful island. Nearby Campbeltown, in Kintyre — once the greatest whisky town of them all — now musters only three malts ... but they are wonderful drams nonetheless.

And finally the Island malts encompass the whiskies of Jura, Mull, Skye and Orkney — each one differing from the other just as the topography of their islands differs. I have also decided to include a malt from Co Antrim in Northern Ireland in this, and all further editions. The reason is simple enough, the whiskey they produce may be in the Irish tradition, but it is a true malt nevertheless and is produced within the confines of the United Kingdom. To ignore it would be to ignore an important contribution to this country's malt whisky heritage.

All this will help to indicate where a whisky comes from and what it tastes like, but I have never been inclined to use the pages of this book as a means of telling the reader how it is made. I have always assumed some foreknowledge of the process but since so many real novitiates, confronted by so much exposure and advertising, are asking how malt is made — and rather than take up space here — I have indicated in the introductory sections to each region where to visit in order to understand the process better. Although there are now some excellent institutions to further one's knowledge there is simply no substitute for visiting a working distillery and being shown round by the very people who make and are proud of their own dram.

SPEYSIDE

For many whisky enthusiasts malt whisky is most closely associated with Speyside, but in truth this is only half the story. The strength of the association, however, can be seen from the many distilleries which, although not situated beside the River Spey, make allegiance with it when stating their provenance.

The River Livet has also suffered from the same back-handed compliment and over the years many distillers (even true Speyside producers) claimed to produce "a Glenlivet", when strictly speaking they were stretching not only the geographical boundaries a bit far, but also the patience of the owners of The Glenlivet Distillery itself. It all goes to show how over the last two centuries "Speyside" has meant high quality, and today the truth of that statement has not diminished at all.

The trade, however, has always tended to look at the large number of distilleries situated in this area as simply "Speysides", and for simplicity's sake I have continued with this categorisation for the Almanac. As you will see from the map over the page, the "Golden Triangle" really exists, stretching from Elgin over towards Banff and down to the cradle of distilling on Speyside — Dufftown. In this triangle lies the greatest concentration of malt whisky-making apparatus in the world, and to savour the atmosphere here is to realise how important and how dearly distilling is held in the Highlands of Scotland. Follow the "Whisky Trail" which is clearly signposted in this area and you will see what I mean.

The success of the Speyside distillers and their current profusion is due to the production of illicit whisky. At the end of the 18th Century, the Highland product was in such demand that the "protected" Lowland markets were infiltrated with the higher quality, smuggled produce of the illicit

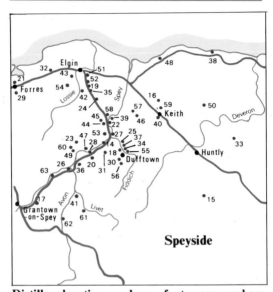

Distillery location numbers refer to page numbers.

still. Finally, in 1823, an Act of Parliament
betrayed the fact that the Government had at last
realised the best way to reduce the illicit trade was
to make it attractive for the distillers to go legal.
The Speyside men were, however, suspicious and
only after George Smith, who distilled in Glenlivet,
went legal in 1824 did they begin to accept the new
laws.

Smith's foresight is manifested in the industry
on Speyside as it stands today. Famous names
abound — Macallan, Cardhu, Linkwood,
Glenfiddich, Mortlach, Tamdhu — each and every
one another experience to savour. Most of these
distilleries can now cater for visitors in a number of
ways and many of them have outstanding facilities
which will not only make a visit to a typical
Speyside distillery something to remember, but
should also give a comprehensive (and
comprehensible!) introduction to the processes

involved in the production of fine malt whisky. Local Tourist Information Centres will be able to give details of their local distilleries with these facilities, but where possible, I have indicated if a distillery can accommodate visitors, and how they can be contacted. Some of the more quick-witted producers like William Grant of Glenfiddich started catering for the visitor some time ago and can offer a day to remember. More recently United Distillers have developed visitor centres of particular appeal at Royal Lochnagar on Deeside, Blair Athol at Pitlochry and Cardhu near Knockando. Wherever you find yourself, be sure to try and visit one of them and buy a bottle of their malt.

Brand	**ABERLOUR**
Distillery	Aberlour ABERLOUR, Banffshire
Status	Subsidiary of Ricard International SA
Reception centre	No
Established	1826
Age when bottled	12 years
Strength	40%

TASTING NOTES

Nose	Rich, delightful, aroma.
Taste	A fine, smooth, lingering texture.
Comments	Good after-dinner dram, becoming popular in France and Italy

PERSONAL NOTES

Malt	**ARDMORE**
Distillery	Ardmore KENNETHMONT, Aberdeenshire
Status	Allied Distillers Ltd
Reception Centre	No
Established	1898-9

TASTING NOTES (18 year old, 46%)

Nose	A light aroma.
Taste	Big, sweet and malty on the palate with a good, crisp finish.
Comments	Only from the independent bottlers (see page 138). After-dinner.

PERSONAL NOTES

Brand	AULTMORE
Distillery	Aultmore KEITH, Banffshire
Status	United Distillers
Reception Centre	No
Established	1896
Age when bottled	12 years
Strength	40%

TASTING NOTES

Nose	A delightful fresh aroma with a sweet hint and a touch of peat.
Taste	Smooth, well balanced with a mellow, warming finish.
Comments	Available readily and suitable as an after-dinner malt.

PERSONAL NOTES

Malt	**BALMENACH**
Distillery	Balmenach Cromdale, GRANTOWN-ON-SPEY, Morayshire
Status	United Distillers
Reception centre	No
Established	c1824

TASTING NOTES (24 year old, 46%)

Nose	Light but attractive.
Taste	Slight spirit flavour with a quick, but full, finish.
Comments	A pre-dinner dram available from the independent bottlers (see page 138).

PERSONAL NOTES

Malt	**THE BALVENIE**
Distillery	Balvenie DUFFTOWN, Banffshire
Status	Wm Grant & Sons Ltd
Reception centre	No, but visitors are always welcome. Tel: 0340-20373.
Established	1892
Age when bottled	The Classic — 12 years minimum Founder's Reserve — 10 years minimum.
Strength	The Classic — 43%, Founder's Reserve — 40%, 43% for export.

TASTING NOTES

Nose	Excellent well-pronounced aroma.
Taste	Big, distinctive flavour with a sweet aftertaste.
Comments	A connoisseur's malt for after-dinner.

PERSONAL NOTES

Malt	**BENRIACH**
Distillery	Benriach Longmorn, ELGIN, Morayshire
Status	The Seagram Co Ltd
Reception centre	No
Established	1898

TASTING NOTES (13 year old, 46%)

Nose	Light, elusive, delicate.
Taste	Medium flavour and taste that takes time to come through on the palate.
Comments	A pre-dinner dram from the independent bottlers (see page 138).

PERSONAL NOTES

Malt	**BENRINNES**
Distillery	Benrinnes ABERLOUR, Banffshire
Status	United Distillers
Reception centre	No
Established	c1835

TASTING NOTES (18 year old, 46%)

Nose	A pleasant delicate hint of peat.
Taste	Subtle, fine flavour which gradually catches up on the tastebuds.
Comments	Pre-dinner, but only available from the independent bottlers (see page 138).

PERSONAL NOTES

Malt	**BENROMACH**
Distillery	Benromach FORRES, Morayshire
Status	United Distillers
Reception Centre	No
Established	1898

TASTING NOTES (14 year old, 46%)

Nose	Light, delicate and attractive.
Taste	Light and delicate but finishes with a pronounced spirit taste.
Comments	Only available from the independent bottlers (see page 138). Pre-dinner.

PERSONAL NOTES

Malt	**CAPERDONICH**
Distillery	Caperdonich ROTHES, Morayshire
Status	The Seagram Co Ltd
Reception centre	No
Established	1898

TASTING NOTES (14 year old, 46%)

Nose	A light, very delicate fragrance of peat.
Taste	Medium, slight hint of fruit with a quick smokey finish.
Comments	Only from the independent bottlers (see page 138). The distillery is across the road from Glen Grant and used to be called Glen Grant No 2.

PERSONAL NOTES

Cardhu Distillery

Brand	CARDHU *(Kaar-doo)*
Distillery	Cardhu KNOCKANDO, Morayshire
Status	United Distillers
Reception centre	Yes. Recently upgraded. Tel: 03406-204
Established	1824
Age when bottled	12 years
Strength	40%

TASTING NOTES

Nose	A hint of sweetness with an excellent bouquet.
Taste	Smooth, mellow flavour with a delightful long-lasting finish.
Comments	Good after-dinner dram, and a malt which is rapidly gaining in popularity.

PERSONAL NOTES

Malt	**COLEBURN**
Distillery	Coleburn Longmorn, ELGIN, Morayshire
Status	United Distillers
Reception centre	No
Established	1897

TASTING NOTES

Nose	Light and flowery.
Taste	Light and pleasant with a well-rounded refreshing aftertaste.
Comments	Only available from the independent bottlers (see page 138).

PERSONAL NOTES

Malt	**CONVALMORE**
Distillery	Convalmore DUFFTOWN, Banffshire
Status	United Distillers
Reception centre	No
Established	1894

TASTING NOTES (19 year old, 46%)

Nose	Delicate and aromatic.
Taste	More pronounced than the aroma suggests. Pleasant roundness and full on the palate.
Comments	An after-dinner malt from the independent bottlers (see page 138).

PERSONAL NOTES

Brand	# CRAGGANMORE
Distillery	Cragganmore BALLINDALLOCH, Banffshire
Status	United Distillers
Reception centre	Yes. Visiting by appointment. Tel: 08072-202
Established	1869-70
Age when bottled	12 years
Strength	40%

TASTING NOTES

Nose	Light delicate aroma.
Taste	Very well balanced distillate with firm body and malty smoke finish on the palate.
Comments	At last available as a brand as part of UD's Classic Malt range.

PERSONAL NOTES

Malt	**CRAIGELLACHIE**
Distillery	Craigellachie CRAIGELLACHIE, Banffshire
Status	United Distillers
Reception centre	No
Established	1891

TASTING NOTES (22 year old, 46%)

Nose	Pungent, smokey.
Taste	Light-bodied, smokey flavour. More delicate on the palate than the nose suggests. Good character.
Comments	After-dinner, but only available from the independent bottlers (see page 138).

PERSONAL NOTES

Malt	**DAILUAINE**
Distillery	Dailuaine CARRON, Morayshire
Status	United Distillers
Reception centre	No, but visitors are welcome
Established	c1852

TASTING NOTES (18 year old, 46%)

Nose	Very pungent and smokey.
Taste	Robust, full of flavour with a lingering finish. Excellent balance of flavour and taste.
Comments	A good after-dinner dram from the independent bottlers (see page 138).

PERSONAL NOTES

Malt	**DALLAS DHU**
	(Dallas-Doo)
Distillery	Dallas Dhu FORRES, Morayshire
Status	United Distillers
Reception centre	Yes. Tel: 0309-76548
Established	1899

TASTING NOTES (21 year old, 46%)

Nose	Delicate touch of peat.
Taste	Full-bodied, lingering flavour and smooth aftertaste.
Comments	The entire distillery is now run by Historic Buildings and Monuments and is an excellent place to visit. An after-dinner dram available from the distillery and the independent bottlers (see page 138).

PERSONAL NOTES

Brand	**DUFFTOWN**
Distillery	Dufftown DUFFTOWN, Banffshire
Status	United Distillers
Reception centre	No
Established	1896
Age when bottled	8 years
Strength	40%

TASTING NOTES

Nose	Light, flowery, pleasant aroma.
Taste	Good, round, smooth taste which tends to linger nicely on the palate.
Comments	Pre-dinner.

PERSONAL NOTES

Brand	**GLENALLACHIE**
Distillery	Glenallachie ABERLOUR, Banffshire
Status	Subsidiary of Ricard International SA
Reception centre	No
Established	1967-8
Age when bottled	12 years
Strength	40%, 43% for export

TASTING NOTES

Nose	Very elegant with a delightful bouquet.
Taste	Smooth bodied with a lovely, light sweet finish. Extremely well balanced.
Comments	Built by W Delmé-Evans for Charles Mackinlay & Co Ltd, this distillery produces one of the most under-rated malts and has recently been acquired by House of Campbell.

PERSONAL NOTES

Brand	**GLENBURGIE**
Distillery	Glenburgie-Glenlivet FORRES, Morayshire
Status	Allied Distillers Ltd
Reception centre	No
Established	1829
Age when bottled	5 years old, but only occasionally available.
Strength	40%

TASTING NOTES (18 year old, 46%)

Nose	A fragrant, herbal aroma.
Taste	A light, delicate, aromatic flavour with a pleasant finish.
Comments	Usually bottled for export only. A good pre-dinner malt.

PERSONAL NOTES

Brand	# GLENDRONACH
Distillery	Glendronach Forgue, by HUNTLY Aberdeenshire
Status	Allied Distillers Ltd
Reception centre	Yes
Established	1826
Age when bottled	12 years (Original & Sherrywood)
Strength	40%, 43% for export

TASTING NOTES (Sherrywood)

Nose	Smooth aroma with a light trace of sweetness.
Taste	Well balanced, lingering on the palate with a delicious, decisive after-taste.
Comments	A good dram, after-dinner. Will definitely be sought after.

PERSONAL NOTES

SINGLE MALT SCOTCH WHISKY
100% SCOTCH WHISKY · PRODUCT OF SCOTLAND
Macdonald Greenlees Ltd.
GLENDULLAN DISTILLERY · DUFFTOWN · SCOTLAND
43% VOL.   CONTENTS 75cl

Brand	**GLENDULLAN**
Distillery	Glendullan DUFFTOWN, Banffshire
Status	United Distillers
Reception centre	Tel: 034385-258
Established	1897-8
Age when bottled	12 years
Strength	43%

TASTING NOTES

Nose	Attractive, fruity bouquet.
Taste	Firm, mellow with a delightful finish and a smooth lingering aftertaste.
Comments	Not very well known, but a good after-dinner malt.

PERSONAL NOTES

Brand	**GLEN ELGIN**
Distillery	Glen Elgin Longmorn, ELGIN, Morayshire
Status	United Distillers
Reception centre	No
Established	1898-1900
Age when bottled	12 years
Strength	43%

TASTING NOTES

Nose	Agreeable aroma of heather and honey.
Taste	Medium-weight touch of sweetness which finishes smoothly.
Comments	The best of both worlds, an excellent all-round malt, suitable for drinking at any time.

PERSONAL NOTES

Brand	**GLENFARCLAS**
Distillery	Glenfarclas Marypark, BALLINDALLOCH Banffshire
Status	J&G Grant
Reception centre	Yes, a very informative one with free tastings
Established	1836
Age when bottled	8, 10, 12, 15, 21 & 25 years
Strength	8 year old — 60% ('105') 10 year old — 40% 15 year old — 46% 12 (export), 21 & 25 year old — 43%

TASTING NOTES *(15 year old, 46%)*

Nose	A rich, delicious promise (which is fulfilled).
Taste	Full of character and flavour, one of the great Highland malts.
Comments	A superb after-dinner dram.

PERSONAL NOTES

Brand	**GLENFIDDICH**
Distillery	Glenfiddich DUFFTOWN, Banffshire
Status	Wm Grant & Sons Ltd
Reception centre	Yes, very popular. Tel: 0340-20373
Established	1886-7
Age when bottled	8 years minimum
Strength	40%

TASTING NOTES

Nose	A light, delicate touch of peat.
Taste	Attractive flavour, with an after-sweetness. Well balanced. A good introductory malt.
Comments	If you have never tasted a malt, start with this one. Glenfiddich has just celebrated its Centenary.

PERSONAL NOTES

Brand	**GLENGLASSAUGH**
Distillery	Glenglassaugh PORTSOY, Banffshire
Status	The Highland Distilleries Co plc
Reception centre	No
Established	1875
Age when bottled	12 years old
Strength	40%

TASTING NOTES

Nose	Light, fresh and delicate
Taste	Charming, a hint of sweetness which is full of promise with a delicious stimulating follow-through.
Comments	For drinking at anytime. Another "newcomer" from Highland Distilleries.

PERSONAL NOTES

Brand	**GLEN GRANT**
Distillery	Glen Grant ROTHES, Morayshire
Status	The Seagram Co Ltd
Reception centre	Yes. Tel: 03403-243
Established	1804
Age when bottled	UK market — none given. Export market — 5 years old (Italy), 10 years old and none given
Strength	40%

TASTING NOTES

Nose	Light, dry aroma.
Taste	Dry flavour, light — another good all-round malt.
Comments	Pre-dinner.

PERSONAL NOTES

Malt	**GLEN KEITH**
Distillery	Glen Keith KEITH, Banffshire
Status	The Seagram Co Ltd
Reception centre	No
Established	1957-60

TASTING NOTES (17 year old, 46%)

Nose	Light, sweet and attractive.
Taste	Light, with a hint of fruit. Smooth and well-rounded.
Comments	Pre-dinner, from the independent bottlers (see page 139).

PERSONAL NOTES

Brand	THE GLENLIVET
Distillery	Glenlivet MINMORE, Banffshire
Status	The Seagram Co Ltd
Reception centre	Yes. Tel: 08073-427
Established	1858
Age when bottled	12 years
Strength	40%, 43% for export

TASTING NOTES

Nose	A light, delicate nose with lots of fruit.
Taste	Medium-light trace of sweetness, quite full on the palate — a first class malt.
Comments	This one never disappoints. Popular and available everywhere.

PERSONAL NOTES

Malt	**GLENLOSSIE**
Distillery	Glenlossie-Glenlivet ELGIN, Morayshire
Status	United Distillers
Reception centre	No
Established	1876

TASTING NOTES (18 year old, 46%)

Nose	Soft touch of sweetness with a suggestion of sandalwood.
Taste	Soft and mellow with a long-lasting aromatic aftertaste.
Comments	Again, only available from the independent bottlers (see page 139).

PERSONAL NOTES

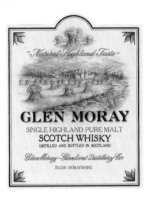

Brand	**GLEN MORAY**
Distillery	Glen Moray ELGIN, Morayshire
Status	Subsidiary of Macdonald Martin Distilleries plc
Reception centre	No
Established	1897
Age when bottled	12 years
Strength	40%

TASTING NOTES

Nose	Fresh, light aroma.
Taste	Light, pleasant and malty with a clean finish. A fine all-round malt.
Comments	A pre-dinner dram, beautifully presented.

PERSONAL NOTES

Brand	# THE GLEN ROTHES
Distillery	Glenrothes ROTHES, MORAYSHIRE
Status	The Highland Distilleries Co plc
Reception centre	No
Established	1878
Age when bottled	12 years old
Strength	43%

TASTING NOTES

Nose	A rich subtle sweetness with a lingering hint of peat-reek.
Taste	A good balance of softness and quality with an exquisite long-lasting flavour.
Comments	After dinner and now available from Berry Bros & Rudd Ltd of *Cutty Sark* fame.

PERSONAL NOTES

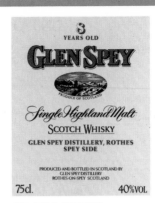

Brand	**GLEN SPEY**
Distillery	Glen Spey ROTHES, Morayshire
Status	International Distillers & Vintners Ltd
Reception centre	No
Established	c1878
Age when bottled	8 years
Strength	40%

TASTING NOTES

Nose	Light, fragrant and delicate.
Taste	Very smooth and fragrant. A good all-round drink.
Comments	Pre-dinner

PERSONAL NOTES

Malt	**GLENTAUCHERS**
Distillery	Glentauchers MULBEN, Banffshire
Status	Allied Distillers Ltd
Reception centre	No
Established	1898

TASTING NOTES (20 year old, 46%)

Nose	Light, sweet aroma.
Taste	Lightly flavoured with a light, dry finish.
Comments	A pre-dinner dram from the independent bottlers (see page 139).

PERSONAL NOTES

Malt	**IMPERIAL**
Distllery	Imperial CARRON, Morayshire
Status	Allied Distillers Ltd
Reception centre	No
Established	1897

TASTING NOTES (1969 distillation)

Nose	Delightful — rich and smokey.
Taste	Rich and mellow with an absolutely delicious finish. A malt of real character.
Comments	After-dinner, again only from the independent bottlers (see page 139).

PERSONAL NOTES

Brand	**INCHGOWER**
Distillery	Inchgower BUCKIE, Banffshire
Status	United Distillers
Reception centre	Provisional
Established	1871
Age when bottled	12 years
Strength	40%

TASTING NOTES

Nose	Very distinctive with a pleasant hint of sweetness.
Taste	Good, distinctive flavour finishing with a light sweetness.
Comments	A well balanced malt. After-dinner.

PERSONAL NOTES

Brand	**KNOCKANDO**
Distillery	Knockando KNOCKANDO, Morayshire
Status	The International Distillers & Vintners Ltd
Reception Centre	No
Established	1898
Age when bottled	10-15 years
Strength •	40%

TASTING NOTES

Nose	Full and pleasant.
Taste	Medium-bodied, with a finish reminiscent of sugar almonds.
Comments	After-dinner. Bottled when it is considered ready, rather than at a pre-determined age. The label carries dates of distillation and bottling.

PERSONAL NOTES

Malt	**KNOCKDHU** *(Knock-doo)*
Distillery	Knockdu KNOCK, Banffshire
Status	Inver House Distillers Ltd
Reception centre	No
Established	1893-4

TASTING NOTES *(1974 distillation)*

Nose	A quite distinctive, dry aroma.
Taste	Medium-bodied, round and gentle on the palate with a pleasant lingering taste.
Comments	After-dinner. Only available from the independent bottlers (see page 139).

PERSONAL NOTES

40%vol PRODUCT OF SCOTLAND 75cl ℮

Brand	**LINKWOOD**
Distillery	Linkwood ELGIN, Morayshire
Status	United Distillers
Reception centre	No. Visiting by appointment. Tel: 0343-7004
Established	c1824
Age when bottled	12 years
Strength	40%

TASTING NOTES

Nose	Slightly smokey with a trace of sweetness.
Taste	Full-bodied hint of sweetness.
Comments	One of the best malts available.

PERSONAL NOTES

Brand	**LONGMORN**
Distillery	Longmorn Longmorn, ELGIN, Morayshire
Status	The Seagram Co Ltd
Reception centre	No
Established	1894-5
Age when bottled	15 years
Strength	43%

TASTING NOTES

Nose	A delightful, fragrant bouquet.
Taste	Full bodied, fleshy, nutty, lots of character.
Comments	Re-introduced at this age in 1986 by marketers Hill, Thomson & Co — at last the public can appreciate this classic after-dinner malt. Outstanding.

PERSONAL NOTES

Brand	# THE MACALLAN
Distillery	Macallan CRAIGELLACHIE, Banffshire
Status	The Macallan Distillers Ltd
Reception centre	Yes. By appointment only
Established	c1824
Age when bottled	UK market — 10, 18 (currently 1968 distillation) and 25 years old. Export market — 10, 12, 18, and 25 years old. Italian market — 7 years old
Strength	7 and 10 year old — 40%, with some 10 year old at 57%; 25 year old, 1968 distillation and export bottlings — 43%.

TASTING NOTES (10 year old)

Nose	Smooth aroma with a silky bouquet.
Taste	Full, delightful and sherried with a beautiful lingering aftertaste.
Comments	A masterpiece. All Macallan is casked in sherrywood.

PERSONAL NOTES

Brand	**MILTON DUFF**
Distillery	Miltonduff-Glenlivet ELGIN, Morayshire
Status	Allied Distillers Ltd
Reception centre	Yes. Tel: 0343-7433
Established	1824
Age when bottled	12 years
Strength	43%

TASTING NOTES

Nose	Agreeable, fragrant bouquet.
Taste	Medium-bodied with a pleasant, well-matured, subtle finish.
Comments	After-dinner. Another malt called *Mosstowie* used to be produced from Lomond type stills at Milton Duff and is available from the independent bottlers (see page 139).

PERSONAL NOTES

Malt	**MORTLACH**
Distillery	Mortlach DUFFTOWN, Banffshire
Status	United Distillers
Reception centre	No
Established	c1823

TASTING NOTES (12 year old, 40%)

Nose	A pleasant, well-rounded aroma.
Taste	Medium-bodied with a well balanced delightful finish.
Comments	A first class after-dinner malt from the independent bottlers (see page 139).

PERSONAL NOTES

Malt	**PITTYVAICH**
Distillery	Pittyvaich DUFFTOWN, Banffshire
Status	United Distillers
Reception centre	No
Established	1974

TASTING NOTES (1976 distillation, 57.7%)

Nose	Rather elegant with a delicate fragrance.
Taste	Mellow and soft with a fulfilling roundness.
Comments	A remarkably good addition to the bottled malts. After dinner, but only available from the independent bottlers (see page 139).

PERSONAL NOTES

Brand	**THE SINGLETON OF AUCHROISK**
Distillery	Auchroisk MULBEN, Banffshire
Status	International Distillers & Vintners Ltd
Reception centre	No
Established	1974
Age when bottled	12 years
Strength	40%

TASTING NOTES

Nose	Distinctive, attractive bouquet with a touch of fruit.
Taste	Medium-weight, hint of sweetness with a delicious long-lasting flavour.
Comments	After-dinner. A new malt from a "new" distillery opened in 1974 and very welcome too. A charmer.

PERSONAL NOTES

Malt	**SPEYBURN**
Distillery	Speyburn ROTHES, Morayshire
Status	United Distillers
Reception centre	No
Established	1897

TASTING NOTES (16 year old, 46%)

Nose	A heather-honey bouquet.
Taste	Big, full-bodied malty taste with a sweet finish.
Comments	After-dinner. From the independent bottlers only (see page 139).

PERSONAL NOTES

Strathisla Distillery

Brand	**STRATHISLA** *(Strath-eyela)*
Distillery	Strathisla KEITH, Banffshire
Status	The Seagram Co Ltd
Reception centre	Yes. Tel: 05422-7471
Established	1786
Age when bottled	12 years
Strength	40%

TASTING NOTES

Nose	Beautiful, bewitching fragrance of fruit which also reflects the taste to come.
Taste	Slender hint of sweetness with an extremely long, lingering fullness. Good balance.
Comments	An excellent after-dinner malt — one of the best to sip and savour. Distilled and bottled by Chivas Brothers Ltd.

PERSONAL NOTES

Brand	**TAMDHU** *(Tamm-doo)*
Distillery	Tamdhu KNOCKANDO, Morayshire
Status	The Highland Distilleries Co plc
Reception centre	Yes. Tel: 03406-221
Established	1896-7
Age when bottled	10 years
Strength	40%

TASTING NOTES

Nose	Light aroma with a trace of sweetness.
Taste	Medium, with a little sweetness and a very mellow finish.
Comments	A good after-dinner dram which is both popular and readily available.

PERSONAL NOTES

Brand	**TAMNAVULIN** *(Tamna-voolin)*
Distillery	Tamnavulin BALLINDALLOCH, Banffshire
Status	The Invergordon Distillers Ltd
Reception centre	Yes. A charming old mill with a beautiful sheltered picnic area
Established	1965-6
Age when bottled	10 years
Strength	40%

TASTING NOTES

Nose	Well matured, mellow, with a hint of sweetness.
Taste	Medium weight with a light, smokey, pronounced finish.
Comments	A good all-round malt.

PERSONAL NOTES

Brand	TOMINTOUL-GLENLIVET *(Tommin-towl)*
Distillery	Tomintoul-Glenlivet BALLINDALLOCH, Banffshire
Status	Whyte & Mackay Distillers Ltd
Reception centre	Tel: 08073-274
Established	1964-5
Age when bottled	None given
Strength	40%, 43% for export

TASTING NOTES

Nose	Light and delicate.
Taste	Light body with good character.
Comments	A good introduction to malt. Bottled in an interesting manner for export.

PERSONAL NOTES

Brand	**TORMORE**
Distillery	Tormore Advie, GRANTOWN-ON-SPEY, Morayshire
Status	Long John International Ltd
Reception centre	No, but visitors are welcome. Tel: 0807-5244
Established	1958-60
Age when bottled	10 years, and 5 for export
Strength	40%, up to 43% for export

TASTING NOTES

Nose	Nicely defined dry aroma.
Taste	Medium-bodied with a hint of sweetness and a pleasant, lingering aftertaste.
Comments	After-dinner.

PERSONAL NOTES

THE HIGHLANDS

Outwith the Speyside area distilling activity is spread more sparsely throughout a wide area which I have taken the liberty to break up into four main regions in the North, South, East and West.

Over 30 malts emanate from these four areas, some sadly from distilleries no longer in existence such as Glen Mhor and Glen Albyn in Inverness, and Glenugie near Peterhead. When you do come across an example of these, remember that you really will be buying a piece of history.

In the far-flung producing localities around the Highlands the importance of the visitor is often keenly felt and despite the travel required to reach these facilities, Highland hospitality still abounds. The existing distilleries in the Northern region stretch from Dalwhinnie near Kingussie to Pulteney at Wick in the north of Caithness and encompass Tomatin at the hamlet of the same name; Royal Brackla near Nairn; Millburn in Inverness; Ord Distillery at Muir of Ord in the Black Isle; Dalmore and Teaninich at Alness; Balblair and Glenmorangie near Tain and Clynelish near Brora. Although most of these malts are not as well known as they should be, many are becoming more popular and none of them should be passed by if you come across them.

The Eastern malts lie between the generalised Speyside region and the North Sea coast. Banff, the fishing town on the Moray Firth possesses two distilleries, though only Glen Deveron is currently in production. The distillery with the town's name has been "mothballed" for some time and the availability of the malt has fluctuated in the recent past. Although Glenugie distillery is defunct, the Peterhead malt can still be found in many specialist shops.

Farming has made the lush lowland area around Aberdeen famous, so it is no surprise to find that at

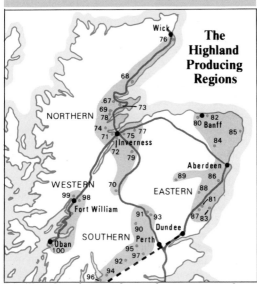

The Highland Producing Regions

Wick 76
68
67
69 — 73
78
NORTHERN
74
71   75 77
72   79
Inverness
82
80 Banff
85
84
Aberdeen
89   86
88
81
WESTERN
99 98
Fort William
70
EASTERN
91   93
90
Dundee
87 83
SOUTHERN
95
92   97
Oban
100
94
96
Perth

Distillery location numbers refer to page numbers.

Glen Garioch waste heat from the direct-fired stills is used to cultivate tomatoes and pot plants. And while Lochnagar cannot offer the visitor such horticultural delights, its new reception centre and proximity to Balmoral Castle make it not only Royal, but a bit special. To the south of Deeside Glenury Royal near Stonehaven and Fettercairn extend the activity to Montrose which boasts a considerable amount of distilling. Glenesk distillery has changed names a few times but its malt remains the same whereas Lochside Distillery (once a brewery) produces both grain and malt whisky. Lochside is very rare and only available from the independent bottlers. Inland, but still on the South Esk river, Brechin has two distilleries at Glencadam and North Port — again both producing quite rare malts. South of this arable region the hills of Perthshire signal the Southern limits of the Highland distilling area.

At Pitlochry, the gateway to the Highlands, the

malt drinker can experience two contrasting distilleries. Edradour is the smallest in Scotland and yet maintains all the advantages of a small 19th century plant, while Blair Athol is a large modern distillery with a brand new reception centre and retail outlet. Aberfeldy Distillery lies at the eastern entrance to the town of the same name on the banks of the River Tay and Glenturret Distillery at Crieff caters for the visitor as well as any distillery can. Tullibardine at Blackford is a "recent" distillery (1948) in a village which also has a mineral water producer and the only commercial malting floors in Scotland built on arguably the oldest brewery site in Scotland! And if that amount of diversity is a surprise, Deanston Distillery on the River Teith at Doune is a converted cotton mill where the vaulted weaving sheds act as bonded warehouses and a small hydro electric generating station is also situated within the plant itself! In the far west of this most southerly of the Highland regions lie Loch Lomond and Glengoyne distilleries. Both almost straddle the Highland line (as does Tullibardine) but claim allegiance to the Highland region. Loch Lomond is a relatively new distillery (1968) which currently produces Inchmurrin malt, whereas Glengoyne has a longer pedigree and resting in a cleft of the Ochil foothills, uniquely caters for visitors with guided tours, retail outlet and a bar with a balcony overlooking a rock pool.

The Western malts are an altogether rarer breed being only three in number. Oban's distillery is situated just off the High Street of this thriving tourist town and is therefore somewhat stretched for visitor facilities, but up the coast at Fort William the mothballed Glenlochy Distillery occupies a site which makes one wonder why the owners have not put it to use attracting tourists. Ben Nevis Distillery on the north of the town is now back in production and is aptly named considering the breathtaking backdrop.

THE NORTHERN HIGHLANDS

Brand	**BALBLAIR**
Distillery	Balblair Edderton, TAIN, Ross-shire
Status	Allied Distillers Ltd
Reception centre	No
Established	c1872
Age when bottled	5 years
Strength	40%

TASTING NOTES

Nose	Delightful, light fragrance of peat.
Taste	Good lingering flavour, long-lasting with a slender hint of sweetness.
Comments	A fine dram anytime. Now bottled by Ballantines and available on the UK market.

PERSONAL NOTES

Brand	**CLYNELISH** *(Kline-leesh).*
Distillery	Clynelish BRORA, Sutherland
Status	United Distillers
Reception centre	No. Visiting by appointment. Tel: 0408-2144
Established	1967-8
Age when bottled	12 years
Strength	40%

TASTING NOTES

Nose	Quite peaty for a Northern malt.
Taste	Rich, pleasant with a slightly dry finish — lots of character.
Comments	Good after-dinner malt. Popular amongst the connoisseurs.

PERSONAL NOTES

Brand	DALMORE
Distillery	Dalmore ALNESS, Ross-shire
Status	Whyte & Mackay Distillers Ltd
Reception centre	No
Established	c1839
Age when bottled	12 years
Strength	40%

TASTING NOTES

Nose	Rich, fresh, with a suggestion of sweetness.
Taste	Full flavour which finishes a touch dry.
Comments	Another really good malt. After-dinner.

PERSONAL NOTES

Brand	**DALWHINNIE**
Distillery	Dalwhinnie DALWHINNIE, Inverness-shire
Status	United Distillers
Reception centre	Provisional. Tel: 05282-264
Established	1897-8
Age when bottled	15 years
Strength	43%

TASTING NOTES

Nose	A gentle aromatic bouquet.
Taste	A luscious flavour with a light honey sweet finish.
Comments	Pre-dinner, and now available as part of UD's Classic Malt range.

PERSONAL NOTES

Malt	**GLEN ALBYN**
Distillery	Glen Albyn INVERNESS, Inverness-shire (Dismantled 1986)
Established	c1846

TASTING NOTES *(20 year old, 46%)*

Nose	Light and smokey. Pleasant.
Taste	Well-rounded, smokey with a full finish.
Comments	Only available from the independent bottlers (see page 138).

PERSONAL NOTES

Dalwhinnie Distillery

Malt	**GLEN MHOR** *(Glen Vawr)*
Distillery	Glen Mhor INVERNESS, Inverness-shire (Dismantled 1986)
Established	1892

TASTING NOTES *(8 year old, 40%)*

Nose	Light, sweet fragrance.
Taste	Light-bodied with a slightly dry finish.
Comments	Good, all-round drinking from the independent bottlers (see page 139).

PERSONAL NOTES

Brand	**GLENMORANGIE**
Distillery	Glenmorangie TAIN, Ross-shire
Status	Subsidiary of Macdonald Martin Distilleries plc
Reception centre	No
Established	1843
Age when bottled	10 years
Strength	40%

TASTING NOTES

Nose	Beautiful aroma. Fresh and sweet with a subtle hint of peat.
Taste	Medium-bodied with a sweet, fresh finish. One to linger and dwell upon.
Comments	An excellent malt, very popular. Remember to pronounce the name as **orangey**. The best-selling malt in Scotland.

PERSONAL NOTES

Brand	**GLENORDIE** *(formerly ORD)*
Distillery	Ord MUIR of ORD, Ross-shire
Status	United Distillers
Reception centre	Yes. Tel: 0463-870421
Established	1838
Age when bottled	12 years
Strength	40%

TASTING NOTES

Nose	A beautifully deep nose, with a tinge of dryness.
Taste	Good depth with a long-lasting, delicious aftertaste. Very smooth.
Comments	After-dinner.

PERSONAL NOTES

Malt	**MILLBURN**
Distillery	Millburn INVERNESS, Inverness-shire
Status	United Distillers
Reception centre	No
Established	c1807

TASTING NOTES (13 year old, 46%)

Nose	A rich aroma with a faint sweetness.
Taste	Full-bodied, a touch of fruit and a good long finish.
Comments	Only from the independent bottlers (see page 139).

PERSONAL NOTES

Malt	**PULTENEY** *(Pult-nay)*
Distillery	Pulteney WICK, Caithness
Status	Allied Distillers Ltd
Reception centre	No
Established	1826

TASTING NOTES (8 year old, 40%)

Nose	Fine, delicate, light aroma with an ozone-like bouquet.
Taste	Light, crisp, refreshing finish.
Comments	An excellent aperitif whisky but only available from the independent bottlers as Old Pulteney (see page 139). The most northerly mainland distillery.

PERSONAL NOTES

Malt	**ROYAL BRACKLA**
Distillery	Royal Brackla NAIRN, Morayshire
Status	United Distillers
Reception centre	No
Established	c1812

TASTING NOTES *(18 year old, 46%)*

Nose	A complex balance of peat and smoke with a touch of sweetness.
Taste	Big, and the peaty-smokey nose comes through on the palate with a hint of fruit and a dry finish.
Comments	An after-dinner dram from the independent bottlers (see page 139).

PERSONAL NOTES

Malt	**TEANINICH**
Distillery	Teaninich ALNESS, Ross-shire
Status	United Distillers
Reception centre	No
Established	1817

TASTING NOTES (26 year old, 46%)

Nose	Subtle, fruity with a gentle bouquet.
Taste	Soft, full of flavour and a delight to drink. Really warms the palate.
Comments	A good pre-dinner malt from the independent bottlers (see page 139).

PERSONAL NOTES

Brand	**TOMATIN**
Distillery	Tomatin TOMATIN, Inverness-shire
Status	Subsidiary of Takara Shuzo & Okura & Co Ltd
Reception centre	Yes. Tel: 08082-234
Established	1897
Age when bottled	5 and 10 years
Strength	40%, 43% for export

TASTING NOTES (10 year old, 40%)

Nose	Pleasant and light.
Taste	Light body, very smooth.
Comments	A pre-dinner dram and a good introduction to malt whisky. The distillery was the first to be acquired by the Japanese in 1985.

PERSONAL NOTES

THE EASTERN HIGHLANDS

Malt	**BANFF**
Distillery	Banff BANFF, Banffshire
Status	United Distillers
Reception centre	No
Established	1863

TASTING NOTES (15 year old, 46%)

Nose	Very light with a trace of smoke.
Taste	Slightly aggressive, finishing a touch fiery. Nonetheless a good bite.
Coimments	Available only from the independent bottlers (see page 138).

PERSONAL NOTES

Malt	**GLENCADAM**
Distillery	Glencadam BRECHIN, Angus
Status	Allied Distillers Ltd
Reception centre	Tel: 03562-2217
Established	c1825

TASTING NOTES (14 year old, 46%)

Nose	Light hint of sweetness.
Taste	Full, with quite a fruity flavour and a good finish.
Comments	An after-dinner malt which is only available from the independent bottlers (see page 139).

PERSONAL NOTES

Brand	**GLEN DEVERON**
Distillery	Macduff BANFF, Banffshire
Status	Subsidiary of General Beverage Corporation, Luxembourg
Reception centre	No
Established	1962-3
Age when bottled	12 years
Strength	40%

TASTING NOTES

Nose	A pronounced, refreshing bouquet.
Taste	Medium weight with a smooth, pleasant flavour and a clean finish.
Comments	After-dinner dram, also available from the independent bottlers as **Macduff** (see page 139).

PERSONAL NOTES

GLENESK

YEARS 12 OLD
SINGLE MALT
HIGHLAND SCOTCH WHISKY

Wm Sanderson Son Ltd.
Distillers, South Queensferry, Scotland
Bottled in Scotland
40% vol   75 cl

Brand	**GLEN ESK**
Distillery	Glen Esk Hillside, MONTROSE, Angus
Status	United Distillers
Reception centre	No
Established	1897
Age when bottled	12 years
Strength	40%

TASTING NOTES

Nose	A light, delicate hint of sweetness.
Taste	Quite full and sweet with a lingering finish, well balanced.
Comments	After-dinner. The distillery was once known as North Esk and also as Hillside.

PERSONAL NOTES

Brand	**GLEN GARIOCH** *(Glen-geerie)*
Distillery	Glen Garioch OLDMELDRUM, Aberdeenshire
Status	Morrison Bowmore Distillers Co Ltd
Reception centre	Yes. Tel: 06512-2706
Established	1798
Age when bottled	10 & 21 years
Strength	10 year old — 40% 21 year old — 43%

TASTING NOTES (21 year old)

Nose	Delicate and smokey.
Taste	Pronounced, peaty flavour with a smooth, pleasant finish.
Comments	Good after-dinner dram, from a distillery which utilises waste heat to cultivate tomatoes and pot-plants!

PERSONAL NOTES

Malt	**GLENUGIE**
Distillery	Glenugie PETERHEAD, Aberdeenshire (no longer licensed)
Established	c1831

TASTING NOTES (20 year old, 46%)

Nose	Hint of ripe fruit.
Taste	Initial trace of sweetness, firm, malty but with a quicky, dry finish.
Comments	Pre-dinner, from the independent bottlers (see page 139).

PERSONAL NOTES

Brand	**GLENURY-ROYAL**
Distillery	Glenury-Royal STONEHAVEN, Kincardineshire
Status	United Distillers
Reception area	No
Established	c1825
Age when bottled	12 years
Strength	40%

TASTING NOTES

Nose	A light hint of smoke with a dry aroma.
Taste	Light body with a dry, smokey finish.
Comments	A good introductory malt, suitable for pre-dinner drinking.

PERSONAL NOTES

Malt	**NORTH PORT**
Distillery	North Port BRECHIN, Angus
Status	United Distillers
Reception centre	No
Established	c1820

TASTING NOTES (17 year old, 46%)

Nose	A rather sharp, pronounced aroma, almost like a pickle.
Taste	Starts sweet, but quickly fades to spirit — quite a sharp tang.
Comments	Pre-dinner, and preferably with water. Available only from the independent bottlers (see page 139).

PERSONAL NOTES

Lochnagar Distillery

Brand	**OLD FETTERCAIRN**
Distillery	Fettercairn FETTERCAIRN, Kincardineshire
Status	Whyte & Mackay Distillers Ltd
Reception centre	Tel: 05614-244
Established	c1824
Age when bottled	None given
Strength	40%

TASTING NOTES

Nose	Light, fresh aroma.
Taste	Fresh, stimulating finish with a touch of dryness.
Comments	A good all-round drink.

PERSONAL NOTES

Brand	ROYAL LOCHNAGAR
Distillery	Lochnagar Crathie, BALLATER, Aberdeenshire
Status	United Distillers
Reception centre	Yes, brand new and worth a visit. Tel: 03384-273.
Established	1826
Age when bottled	12 years
Strength	40%

TASTING NOTES

Nose	Pleasant, full nose.
Taste	Good, full body with a clean, wholesome taste. Delicious trace of sweetness.
Comments	After-dinner and favoured by Queen Victoria who frequently took whisky in her tea!

PERSONAL NOTES

THE SOUTHERN HIGHLANDS

Malt	**ABERFELDY**
Distillery	Aberfeldy ABERFELDY, Perthshire
Status	United Distillers
Reception centre	Yes. Tel: 0887-20330
Established	c1830

TASTING NOTES (1969 distillation)

Nose	Fresh, clean with a lightly peated nose.
Taste	Nice substantial flavour with a good round taste.
Comments	From the independent bottlers (see page 138).

PERSONAL NOTES

Blair Athol Distillery

Brand	**BLAIR ATHOL**
Distillery	Blair Athol PITLOCHRY, Perthshire
Status	United Distillers
Reception centre	Yes, with good facilities for trade and public. Tel: 0796-2234.
Established	1879
Age when bottled	8 years
Strength	40%

TASTING NOTES

Nose	Light, fresh, clean aroma.
Taste	Medium hint of peat with a nice round finish. Plenty of flavour.
Comments	Pre-dinner, readily available.

PERSONAL NOTES

Brand	**DEANSTON**
Distillery	Deanston DOUNE, Perthshire
Status	The Invergordon Distillers Ltd
Reception centre	No
Established	1965-6
Age when bottled	None given
Strength	40%

TASTING NOTES

Nose	A hint of sweetness.
Taste	Light, finishing with a smooth trace of the same.
Comments	A pre-dinner malt, from a distillery which used to be a cotton mill until 1965 and boasts not only vaulted bonds, which were formerly the weaving sheds, but also its own hydro-elecric generating station!

PERSONAL NOTES

Brand	**EDRADOUR**
	(Edra-dower)
Distillery	Edradour
	PITLOCHRY, Perthshire
Status	Subsidiary of Ricard
	International SA
Reception centre	Yes. Tel: 0796-2095
Established	c1837
Age when bottled	10 years
Strength	40%

TASTING NOTES *(18 year old, 46%)*

Nose	Fruity-sweet and smokey.
Taste	Creamy, smooth and malty with a tinge of dryness and a good aftertaste.
Comments	Scotland's smallest distillery and therefore closest to a working 19th-century distillery. Well worth a visit to see how it used to be done.

PERSONAL NOTES

Brand	# GLENGOYNE
Distillery	Glengoyne DUMGOYNE, Stirlingshire
Status	Lang Brothers Ltd
Reception centre	Yes. Tel: 041-332-6361
Established	c1833
Age when bottled	10, 12 & 17 years
Strength	10 year old — 40% 12 year old (Export & Duty Free) — 43% 17 year old — 43%

TASTING NOTES (10 year old)

Nose	A light, fresh aroma.
Taste	Light, pleasant all-round malt.
Comments	Another great introduction to malts. The newly-introduced 17 year old will gain many friends.

PERSONAL NOTES

Brand	# THE GLENTURRET
Distillery	Glenturret The Hosh, CRIEFF, Perthshire
Status	Subsidiary of Cointreau, SA
Reception centre	Yes. Very popular Award Winning Heritage Centre with audio-visual, Exhibition Museum, tasting bar and restaurant.
Established	1775
Age when bottled	8, 12, 15 and 21 years
Strength	40%

TASTING NOTES (12 year old)

Nose	Very impressive aromatic nose.
Taste	Full, lush body with a good depth of flavour and a stimulating finish. Delightful.
Comments	An award-winning malt from arguably Scotland's oldest distillery, where the cat 'Towser', which died aged 23 in March 1987, held the world record for catching mice — over 27,890!

PERSONAL NOTES

Brand	# INCHMURRIN
Distillery	Loch Lomond ALEXANDRIA, Dunbartonshire
Status	Glen Catrine Bonded Warehouse Ltd
Reception centre	No
Established	1965-6
Age when bottled	None given
Strength	40%

TASTING NOTES

Nose	Slightly aromatic. Follows through on the palate.
Taste	Light bodied. Most of the flavour is on the front of the palate and thus finishes quickly.
Comments	A good everyday drinking malt. Pre-dinner. Formerly owned by ADP and then Inver House Distillers, the distillery now produces two malts from stills similar to those at Littlemill.

PERSONAL NOTES

PRODUCT OF SCOTLAND

Tullibardine

SINGLE HIGHLAND MALT SCOTCH WHISKY

A Single Malt Scotch Whisky of quality and distinction distilled and bottled by
TULLIBARDINE DISTILLERY LIMITED
BLACKFORD   PERTHSHIRE   SCOTLAND

40% VOL   750 ML

Brand	**TULLIBARDINE** *(Tully-bardeen)*
Distillery	Tullibardine BLACKFORD, Perthshire
Status	The Invergordon Distillers Ltd
Reception centre	No
Established	1949
Age when bottled	10 years
Strength	40%

TASTING NOTES

Nose	Delicate, mellow, sweet aroma.
Taste	Full-bodied, with a fruity flavour and a good lingering taste.
Comments	A pre-dinner dram from another distillery designed by W Delme-Evans.

PERSONAL NOTES

THE WESTERN HIGHLANDS

Malt	**BEN NEVIS**
Distillery	Ben Nevis FORT WILLIAM, Inverness-shire
Status	Nikka Distillers, Japan
Reception centre	No
Established	c1825

TASTING NOTES (19 year old, 46%)

Nose	Curious, ripe fruit nose.
Taste	Round flavour of no great character but good for beginners.
Comments	Tasting sample not typical of the current product. From the independent bottlers (see page 138). The distillery was purchased by Nikka in early 1989.

PERSONAL NOTES

Malt	# GLENLOCHY
Distillery	Glenlochy FORT WILLIAM, Inverness-shire
Status	United Distillers
Reception centre	No
Established	1898

TASTING NOTES (26 year old, 46%)

Nose	Light and aromatic.
Taste	Light, spicy flavour which tends to finish quickly.
Commetns	Pre-dinner drinking, but only from the independent bottlers (see page 139). The distillery is delightfully situated on the edge of the town.

PERSONAL NOTES

43% vol   75 cl ℮

Brand	**OBAN**
Distillery	Oban OBAN, Argyll
Status	United Distillers
Reception centre	Yes. Tel: 0631-62110
Established	c1794
Age when bottled	14 years
Strength	43%

TASTING NOTES

Nose	Fresh hint of peat.
Taste	Firm, malty flavour finishing very smoothly. Quite silky.
Comments	One of UD's Classic Malt range. An excellent anytime dram from a distillery founded by the Stevensons.

PERSONAL NOTES

THE LOWLANDS

The modern difference between Lowland malt and that originating from the other regions is simply one of style. Historically, the distinguishing factors were more numerous. In the late 18th century the product of the discreet Highland still (be it legal or illegal) was considered a wholesome, hand-crafted product which was in great demand in the urban markets, but the larger Lowland distillers produced a relatively coarse whisky (rarely made purely from malted barley alone) in huge industrial stills in an effort to supply both the city drinkers and the lucrative London market. This distinction was created by the industrial Lowland distillers who aggressively exploited whatever Government legislation was in force. The distinctions were magnified by the drawing of the "Highland Line" which effectively stretched from Greenock on the Clyde to Dundee on the Tay and split the country into two regions gauged by two separate sets of Excise regulations due to the disparity between their respective products.

Eventually the technical differences were removed when more realistic early-19th century Government Acts encouraged illicit distillers in the Highlands to go legal and allowed all producers to distil on a more equal basis. The massive grain distilleries of the central belt may be fewer now but they are still the sole remaining throwback to the days when the Steins and the Haigs wielded some of the most powerful industrial might in Scotland.

Although there is now a relatively low amount of distilling in the Lowlands, small malt distilleries were once in abundance even in the late 19th century. In the remote south west corner, over a dozen concerns existed stretching from Stranraer to Annan. Only Bladnoch Distillery survives and although the substantial remains of two distilleries at Langholm and Annan can still be viewed the

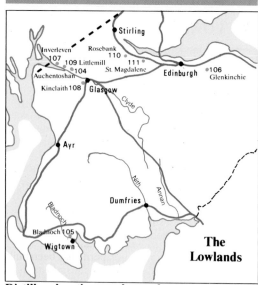

Inverleven
•107
Stirling
Rosebank
110
109 Littlemill 111
104   St. Magdalene
Auchentoshan   Edinburgh   •106
                                      Glenkinchie
Kinclaith 108 Glasgow
                        Clyde
            Ayr
                    Nith Annan
                Dumfries
        Bladnoch
    Bladnoch 105
    Wigtown

**The
Lowlands**

Distillery location numbers refer to page numbers.
malt they once produced has long been drunk
away.

    Fortunately we can still sample many good
malts in the Lowland region. Scotland's most
southerly is produced at Bladnoch, a beautifully
located distillery with a new reception centre which
is well worth the drive from Dumfries along the
famous Solway coast. Just up the road from
Bladnoch, at Girvan on the Ayrshire coast the less
famous Ladyburn malt is produced beside Wm
Grant's grain whisky distillery. Although bottled
for export it can be obtained from the independent
bottlers as well.

    But most of the Lowland malts are produced
to the north along the Highland line. In the
Glasgow area, a visit to one of the malt distilleries
near the city should not be missed. Just north of the
Clyde along the A82 route to Loch Lomond lies
Auchentoshan Distillery, which is one of the two
Lowland distilleries still employing the technique

of triple-distillation. This distillery caters well for the visitor with one of the first reception centres to be established in Scotland. Littlemill Distillery lies nearby, and employed triple distillation until the 1930's. Kinclaith malt still exists although the distillery is now no longer in existence having once been part of Long John's Strathclyde grain distilling complex. Another malt in a similar position is Inverleven which emanates from the curious Lomond stills at the malt distillery within Hiram Walker's vast grain distillery at Dumbarton. Rosebank, which lies nearer Edinburgh at Falkirk, is similar to Auchentoshan in that it too employs triple distillation and the result is one of the great Lowland malts, highly regarded as a pre-dinner dram and a wonderful surprise to anyone drinking their first malt whisky. Not far away, at Linlithgow, St Magdalene is currently "mothballed".

Much of Edinburgh's prosperity has been built on brewing and distilling although the industry is greatly reduced within the city now. There are no malt distilleries operating within the city and all activity is concentrated in producing grain whisky. However, to the east of the city Glenkinchie Distillery at Pencaitland was one of the first to cater for visitors. It also has an interesting collection of museum pieces and gives a thorough insight into the "tools of the trade". This malt is now bottled as a brand under the Classic Malt banner by UD, but all of them are worth looking out for and give a good indication of the Lowland style — light, fragrant and an excellent way to start drinking malt whisky.

Brand	# AUCHENTOSHAN
Distillery	Auchentoshan DUNTOCHER, Dunbartonshire
Status	Morrison Bowmore Distillers Ltd
Reception centre	Yes, currently handling 40,000 visitors per annum and to be expanded. Tel: 03897-8561.
Established	c1800
Age when bottled	5, 10, 12 & 18 years
Strength	40%, 43% for export

TASTING NOTES (10 year old)

Nose	Delicate, slightly sweet.
Taste	Light, soft sweetness with a good aftertaste.
Comments	A triple-distilled malt from one of Scotland's most visited distilleries. Popular and readily available at home and abroad. If you're in Glasgow, drop in for a dram.

PERSONAL NOTES

Brand	**BLADNOCH**
Distillery	Bladnoch BLADNOCH, Wigtownshire
Status	United Distillers
Reception centre	Yes. A charming place to visit. Tel: 09884-2235.
Established	1817
Age when bottled	8 years
Strength	40%

TASTING NOTES

Nose	Very light and delicate.
Taste	Smooth, delicate but full and easy to drink.
Comments	Scotland's most southerly distillery. A pre-dinner malt gaining in popularity since acquisition by Arthur Bell in 1983.

PERSONAL NOTES

Brand	**GLENKINCHIE**
Distillery	Glenkinchie PENCAITLAND, East Lothian
Status	United Distillers
Reception centre	Yes, and a museum. Tel: 0875-34033
Established	c1837
Age when bottled	10 years
Strength	43%

TASTING NOTES

Nose	Light fragrant sweetness.
Taste	Round flavour, slightly dry with a lingering smoothness.
Comments	An excellent pre-dinner dram, now available as part of UD's Classic Malt range.

PERSONAL NOTES

Malt	**INVERLEVEN**
Distillery	Inverleven DUMBARTON, Strathclyde
Status	Allied Distillers Ltd
Reception centre	No
Established	1938

TASTING NOTES (17 year old, 46%)

Nose	Delicate hint of smoke.
Taste	Quite full-bodied. Smooth, with a round palate.
Comments	Rarely available unless obtained from the independent bottlers (see page 139).

PERSONAL NOTES

Malt	# KINCLAITH
Distillery	Kinclaith (dismantled 1975)
Established	1957-8

TASTING NOTES (18 year old, 46%)

Nose	Light and smokey with a spirit sharpness.
Taste	Full-bodied, smooth with an attractive finish.
Comments	From the independent bottlers (see page 139).

PERSONAL NOTES

Brand	# LITTLEMILL
Distillery	Littlemill BOWLING, Dunbartonshire
Status	Barton International Ltd
Reception centre	No
Established	1772
Age when bottled	5 and 8 years
Strength	40%

TASTING NOTES (8 year old)

Nose	Light and delicate.
Taste	Mellow-flavoured, light, slightly cloying yet pleasant and warming.
Comments	Pre-dinner, from a distillery full of interesting, novel features. Certainly one of the oldest in Scotland.

PERSONAL NOTES

Brand	**ROSEBANK**
Distillery	Rosebank Camelon, FALKIRK Stirlingshire
Status	United Distillers
Reception centre	No. Visiting by appointment. Tel: 0324-23325.
Established	c1840
Age when bottled	8 years
Strength	40%

TASTING NOTES

Nose	Light, yet delicate.
Taste	Well balanced, good flavour with entirely acceptable astringency.
Comments	A triple-distilled malt suitable for pre-dinner drinking.

PERSONAL NOTES

Malt	**ST MAGDALENE**
Distillery	St Magdalene LINLITHGOW, West Lothian
Status	United Distillers
Reception centre	No
Established	c1798

TASTING NOTES (20 year old, 46%)

Nose	A round aroma with a touch of smoke.
Taste	Full-bodied, smooth with a ripe finish and much character.
Comments	After-dinner malt. Again only from the independent bottlers (see page 139).

PERSONAL NOTES

ISLAY

O f all Scotland's malts, the Islays are perhaps the most easily recognised. But even so, there are some surprises within this group which are traditionally held to be amongst the heaviest and most pungent available. Their most recognisable characteristics are due to production methods which were developed in concert with the available distilling ingredients in this remote locality. While the mainland markets were supplied by mainland distillers in the 18th and 19th centuries, the islanders supplied a local market from stills — both legal and illegal — which were operated from farmyards, bothies on the bleak moors above Port Ellen and remote caves along the precipitous coast of the Oa.

Islay, renowned as the most fertile island in the Hebrides, had three major assets in this development, a ready source of local barley — or bere as it was then known — inexhaustible amounts of peat and burns running brim-full of soft water. Coupled to this was the likelihood that the art of distilling was probably brought to Scotland via Islay by the Irish in the 15th century. It is impossible to visit Islay and not notice the peat. Along the roadside crossing the enormous Laggan Bog between Port Ellen and Bowmore the peat banks spread as far as the eye can see. This fuel was the only means by which the islanders could dry their grain which was an essential process not only for distilling but also for storage during the wet seasons. By kilning barley it could be kept longer and the dryer the grain was, the less likely it was to go mouldy.

As the grain dried in the fumes, the peat imparted to the barley a highly distinctive character which manifested itself when the spirit was finally distilled from it. These characteristics are still apparent in today's Islay malts and are best

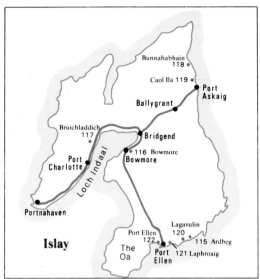

Bunnahabhain 118

Caol Ila 119

Port Askaig

Ballygrant

Bruichladdich 117

Bridgend

Port Charlotte

116 Bowmore
Bowmore

Loch Indaal

Portnahaven

Islay

The Oa

Lagavulin 120

Port Ellen 122

115 Ardbeg

Port Ellen

121 Laphroaig

Distillery location numbers refer to page numbers.

experienced by trying Ardbeg, Lagavulin and Laphroaig which form the three most traditional Islay malts. The other Islays display this peaty-smokey characteristic to a lesser degree but it is always detectable nonetheless.

It is good to see that the Islay distillers — despite their more remote location — are always able to accommodate visitors and some of the distilleries are spectacularly situated. All of them have one thing in common — they are built on the seashore. A century ago this afforded them the access to the sea and thus the mainland markets. The smaller inland farmyard distilleries had by then been unable to compete and one by one they closed down. But it is still possible to see the sites of these traditional distilleries, most notably at Octomore Farm behind Port Charlotte, at Tallant Farm above Bowmore and at Lossit Kennels by Bridgend. Of the present distilleries perhaps

Bowmore is most favourably endowed for the visitor. Not only does it produce a memorable dram but it has a superb reception centre and is shortly to construct a swimming pool in one of its old bonded warehouses for the local community. In the south of the island Lagavulin and Laphroaig both cater well for the visitor and are magnificently located by the sea. Ardbeg — although sadly still closed — is a more sobering prospect given that the distillery was once the centre of a large community. Similarly Port Ellen is closed but the associated maltings are at last being put to better use and are supplying not only Lagavulin and Caol Ila with malt, but also some of the other non-UD distilleries on the island.

Across Loch Indaal from Bowmore lies Bruichladdich which, like Bunnahabhain, produces one of the lighter Islays. This distillery was one of the first in the Hebrides to be constructed from concrete in 1881. Near Port Askaig, at the point where you cross to Jura, lie Caol Ila and Bunnahabhain with spectacular views of the Paps of Jura. Caol Ila is as modern and efficient a distillery as you are likely to find and the stillhouse alone is worth seeing. The dram is not readily available but it is a good Islay as is its close neighbour which was built in 1880-1. Bunnahabhain is for many people the best introduction to the Islays since it is neither too heavy nor too light, and for many newcomers to the Islays it remains their favourite dram.

A trip around Scotland's malts cannot be considered complete unless the Islays are undertaken with fervour for it is in their makeup that the blender finds his greatest inspiration, the enthusiast finds his greatest experience and the taster finds his greatest joy.

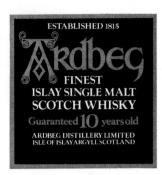

Brand	**ARDBEG**
Distillery	Ardbeg PORT ELLEN, Islay, Argyll
Status	Allied Distillers Ltd
Reception centre	No
Established	c1794
Age when bottled	10 years
Strength	40%

TASTING NOTES

Nose	Lovely peaty aroma with a hint of sweetness.
Taste	Full-bodied and luscious with an excellent aftertaste.
Comments	Good after-dinner malt. Perhaps the ultimate test for beginners?

PERSONAL NOTES

Brand	**BOWMORE**
Distillery	Bowmore BOWMORE, Islay, Argyll
Status	Morrison Bowmore Distillers Ltd
Reception centre	Yes, the best in the islands. Tel: 049681-441
Established	c1770
Age when bottled	10 & 12 years
Strength	40%, 43% for export

TASTING NOTES

Nose	Light, peaty-smokey.
Taste	Healthy, middle-range Islay with medium weight and a smooth finish.
Comments	Very popular after-dinner malt. Some of the older sherry-casked bottlings are outstanding. Distillery is well worth visiting and is about to convert a bonded warehouse into a swimming pool heated from the stillhouse!

PERSONAL NOTES

Brand	**BRUICHLADDICH** *(Broo-ick-laddie)*
Distillery	Bruichladdich BRUICHLADDICH, Islay Argyll
Status	The Invergordon Distillers Ltd
Reception centre	No, but visitors are always welcome. Tel: 049685-221
Established	1881
Age when bottled	10 years
Strength	40%

TASTING NOTES

Nose	Light to medium with a hint of peat.
Taste	Lingering flavour giving the expected fullness of Islay character whilst lacking the heavier tones.
Comments	A good pre-dinner dram.

PERSONAL NOTES

Brand	# BUNNAHABHAIN *(Bu-na-ha-van)*
Distillery	Bunnahabhain PORT ASKAIG, Islay, Argyll
Status	The Highland Distilleries Co plc
Reception centre	No, but visitors are always welcome. Tel: 049684-646
Established	1880-1
Age when bottled	12 years
Strength	40%

TASTING NOTES

Nose	Pronounced character with a flowery aroma.
Taste	Not reminiscent of the Islay style, but a lovely round flavour nonetheless.
Comments	A popular after-dinner dram gaining new friends in France and the United States.

PERSONAL NOTES

Malt	**CAOL ILA** *(Koal-eela)*
Distillery	Caol Ila PORT ASKAIG, Islay, Argyll
Status	United Distillers
Reception centre	No. Visiting by appointment. Tel: 049684-207
Established	1846

TASTING NOTES (1969 distillation)

Nose	Light, fresh with a trace of peat.
Taste	Not a heavy Islay, but has pleasing weight and a fairly round flavour. Finishes smoothly.
Comments	Popular pre-dinner dram, readily available from the independent bottlers (see page 138). Distillery is spectacularly situated on the Sound of Islay.

PERSONAL NOTES

Caol Ila stillhouse

LAGAVULIN

SINGLE ISLAY MALT WHISKY

AGED **16** YEARS

SCOTCH WHISKY

Moss water, passing over rocky falls, steeped in mountain air and moorland peat, distilled and matured in oak casks exposed to the sea shape Lagavulin's robust and smoky character. Time, say the Islanders, TAKES OUT THE FIRE but LEAVES IN THE WARMTH.

"THE STRANGE HORSE OF SUINABHAL" – By William Black. – "I hef been in Isla more as three times or two times myself, and I hef been close to the 'Lagavulin 'Distillery, and I know that it is the clear watter of the spring that will make the 'Lagavulin 'Whisky just as fine as new milk."

75 cl ℮   White Horse Distillers Limited Glasgow   43% vol

ISLAND of ISLAY

Brand	**LAGAVULIN** *(Lagga-voolin)*
Distillery	Lagavulin PORT ELLEN, Islay, Argyll
Status	United Distillers
Reception centre	Yes. Visiting by appointment. Tel: 0496-2400.
Established	1816
Age when bottled	16 years
Strength	43%

TASTING NOTES

Nose	A typical Islay — heavy, powerful aroma. Unmistakable.
Taste	Quite heavy and very full with a delightful hint of sweetness at this age.
Comments	Newly introduced into UD's Classic Malt range. A gentle giant of a dram. One of the best.

PERSONAL NOTES

LAPHROAIG®

SINGLE ISLAY MALT
SCOTCH WHISKY

10
Years Old

The most richly flavoured of
all Scotch whiskies

ESTABLISHED
1815

DISTILLED AND BOTTLED BY

D. JOHNSTON & CO., LAPHROAIG, LAPHROAIG DISTILLERY, ISLE OF ISLAY.

40% vol   75 cl

Brand	**LAPHROAIG** *(La-froyg)*
Distillery	Laphroaig PORT ELLEN, Islay, Argyll
Status	Long John International Ltd
Reception centre	No, but visitors are always welcome. Tel: 0496-2418.
Established	1826
Age when bottled	10 and 15 years
Strength	40%, up to 45.1% for export.

TASTING NOTES (10 year old)

Nose	Well balanced, peaty-smokey.
Taste	Full of character, big Islay peaty flavour with a delightful touch of sweetness. Betrays its proximity to the sea.
Comments	An excellent after dinner malt from a beautifully situated distillery. Very popular.

PERSONAL NOTES

Malt	**PORT ELLEN**
Distiller	Port Ellen PORT ELLEN, Islay, Argyll
Status	United Distillers
Reception cente	No
Established	1825

TASTING NOTES (1969 distillation)

Nose	A hint of peat with a delicate bouquet.
Taste	Light for an Islay lacking that characteristic peaty flavour. A dry finish.
Comments	A popular pre-diner dram from the independent bottlers (see page 139). Direct exports to the Americas were first pioneered at Port Ellen in the 1840s.

PERSONAL NOTES

CAMPBELTOWN

Dufftown could lay claim to being Scotland's whisky capital but in the middle of the last century there was only one place which had the right to that name — Campbeltown. Situated on the lee shore of the Mull of Kintyre, this town was literally awash with distillate a hundred years ago. When Alfred Barnard compiled his wonderful book — *The Whisky Distilleries of the United Kingdom* in 1886, he found no less than 21 producing distilleries in and around the town!

The number of operations were a throwback to the days when illicit distillation in the district was rife, and was not entirely discouraged by the landowners. Campbeltown's boom period was based upon a ready and huge market in cheap Scotch within the working population in the industrial central belt and the avaricious desire of the distillers to supply that market come what may. A local coal seam seemed perfect as a cheap source of fuel, but its exhaustion was to prove fatal, and as the late Victorian boom in whisky distilling collapsed so too did distilling in Campbeltown. The sad reminder of the industry's presence in the town is now manifested in two distilleries, Glen Scotia and Springbank, of which only the latter is still producing at the moment.

It would be unwise to forget Campbeltown's contribution to distilling despite the fact that it is unlikely more distilleries will ever start up in the town again. Its product had a unique regional flavour which came close to the Islay style. This can still be found in Longrow, a traditional old-fashioned malt which is distilled at Springbank. Its character differs from its sister malt Springbank which is a smoother, more elegant dram — one which has become phenomenally successful in Japan where it outsells all the others. That is has succeeded so well is a tribute to the family which

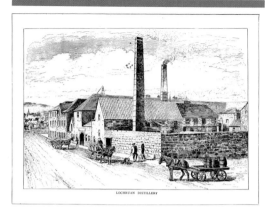

LOCHRUAN DISTILLERY

has always owned the distillery and which has always recognised its quality.

The drawings which appear here show something of the nature of distilling operations in the 'good old days' in the 1880's. When Barnard visited the town he noted that "... Sunday in Campbeltown is carried to its Jewish length, and is quite a day of gloom and penance ... it is said that there are as many places of worship as distilleries in the town". His remarks, no matter how flippant, are important since they set down a precise record of the "Golden Age" of distilling in Scotland — a time we are unlikely to experience again. If Campbeltown's decline has served any purpose at all, it will have been to remind us all of the fickle nature of the marketplace.

As a town, Campbeltown is delightfully situated. Its remoteness allows its inhabitants a certain privacy from the mainstream tourist traffic during summer, but it is always worth considering the detour down the Mull of Kintyre when travelling through this part of the world. The overwhelming impression is that of a thriving fishing and market town, but the names of old distilleries are to be found in a number of nameplaces — Ardlussa, Lochruan, Dalintober and

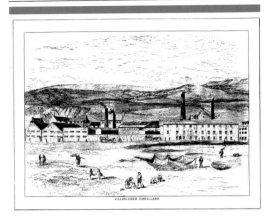

DALINTOBER DISTILLERY.

the like. Savour them as you savour a dram in this setting — I have always said that drinking malt at source is the best way to appreciate it. Try it in Campbeltown.

Brand	**GLEN SCOTIA**
Distillery	Glen Scotia CAMPBELTOWN, Argyll
Status	Barton International Ltd
Reception centre	No
Established	c1832
Age when bottled	8 years
Strength	40%

TASTING NOTES

Nose	Faint touch of smoke. Intense aroma, but still delicate and sweet.
Taste	Light for a Campbeltown. Hint of peat with a good finish.
Comments	Pre-dinner dram. In fact, a good drink at any time.

PERSONAL NOTES

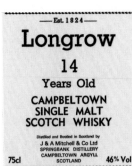

Brand	**LONGROW**
Distillery	Springbank CAMPBELTOWN, Argyll
Status	J&A Mitchell & Co Ltd
Reception centre	No
Established	c1824
Age when bottled	16 years old, (export also)
Strength	46%

TASTING NOTES

Nose	Peaty, smokey.
Taste	Well balanced, with a hint of sweetness. A creamy, malty palate and a fine lingering aftertaste. Almost an Islay.
Comments	Distilled at Springbank, but by using entirely peat-dried malted barley, the heavier peated malt results. A dram for the coinnoisseur.

PERSONAL NOTES

Brand	# SPRINGBANK
Distillery	Springbank CAMPBELTOWN, Argyll
Status	J&A Mitchell & Co Ltd
Reception centre	No
Established	c1830
Age when bottled	12, 15, 21, 25 & 30 years. Export: 8, 10, 15, 21 & 33 years.
Strength	12, 15, 21 & 30 years old — 46%; 12 year old— 57%. Export: 8, 10, 15 & 21 years old — 43%; 33 year old — 46%

TASTING NOTES (21 year old, 46%)

Nose	Steadfast, with a pronounced aroma and a slight sweetness.
Taste	Well balanced, full of charm and elegance. A malt drinker's dream.
Comments	Largest selling malt in Japan and a classic for the malt lover. Superb after-dinner drink — you won't refuse the second one! Bottled at the distillery and now widely available.

PERSONAL NOTES

THE ISLANDS AND N. IRELAND

Recent archaeological finds on the island of Rhum in the Inner Hebrides suggest that the natives knew how to make a brew long before the Irish were credited with introducing the art of distillation to their Scottish cousins. Wm Grant & Son Ltd (makers of Balvenie and Glenfiddich) even went so far as to try and recreate the original 4000 year old recipe which was scientifically reconstructed from scrapings off pottery shards. The brew was drawn from local herbs, grasses and other vegetation and turned out to be a little immature, but like all good brews it improved with familiarity. The last two centuries may have gradually familiarised the world to Scotch, but we can now lay claim to having played a fundamental part in the history of the development of distillation. And for the present-day visitor to Scotland, the past is manifested in some of the most gloriously situated distilleries in the world.

The styles of these malts differ, partly due to location and partly due to the desires of the distillery operators. For instance Jura, from the island just north of Islay, can be fairly described as a Highland-like dram whereas in the last century it was much closer in style to its Islay neighbours. The reason is that the distillery went out of production in 1901 and was replaced in 1963 with a completely new unit designed by W Delmé-Evans. He had stills of a highland-type design installed and used malt that was only lightly peated. Similarly Tobermory's distillery has had its plant changed over the years and has produced some variable distillations of Ledaig until ceasing production in 1980.

On Skye an altogether more traditional taste is found. Talisker is one of the giants among malt. It is a 'big' whisky in every way with an explosive effect on the palate and a wonderful, peaty, sweetness on the nose. The distillery has changed considerably

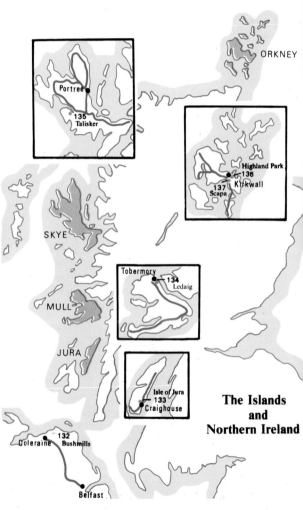

ORKNEY

Portree

135
Talisker

Highland Park
136
Kirkwall
137
Scapa

SKYE

Tobermory
134
Ledaig

MULL

JURA

Isle of Jura
133
Craighouse

The Islands
and
Northern Ireland

132
Coleraine   Bushmills

Belfast

Distillery location numbers refer to page numbers.

but still retains some of the more traditional implements associated with 18th and 19th century distilling. For instance, swan-necked lyne arms can be seen dropping into wooden worm tubs outside the stillhouse wall — the same technique illicit distillers used though on a much smaller scale. Talisker's taste is perhaps the most recognisable among the island and western malts and should benefit greatly from the greater exposure it will undoubtedly receive from its new-look packaging and presentation.

Orkney is the most northerly outpost of whisky distilling in Scotland with two very good malts emanating from Highland Park and Scapa. The surrounding Orcadian landscape at first sight appears bleak but its loveliness grows on the visitor just as their malts do. Their style is traditional — they are both very silky in texture and have a very faithful following among enthusiasts.

At the other geographical extreme across the North Channel from Galloway and only 17 miles (27 Km) from Islay's southern shore lies another island — Ireland. Here, in County Antrim the oldest whiskey distillery in the world is producing a malt whiskey at Bushmills. It would be a nonsense to say it does not have a place in this book given that Islay (and therefore Scotland) probably owes much of its distilling heritage to Ireland. This dram is a pleasant surprise and should not be missed out. Within it I can detect subtle inferences from Islay, Campbeltown and Galloway and as such it should be accepted as part of the family. Notwithstanding that, the island malts show a tremendous variance in style and texture and are a good way to start an education of what is available to the malt drinker. To anyone who thinks that all malt whisky tastes the same, the island drams are a perfect answer.

Brand	**BUSHMILLS**
Distillery	Bushmills BUSHMILLS, Co Antrim N Ireland
Status	Irish Distillers Ltd
Reception centre	Yes. Very popular. Advisable to telephone in advance. Tel: 02657-31521
Established	1608
Age when bottled	10 years
Strength	40%

TASTING NOTES

Nose	Light, smokey, fragrant aroma.
Taste	Reflects the aroma. A very attractive lingering aftertaste of a well matured malt.
Comments	The only Irish malt whiskey from the oldest whiskey distillery in the world.

PERSONAL NOTES

Brand	**ISLE OF JURA**
Distillery	Isle of Jura Craighouse, JURA, Argyll
Status	The Invergordon Distillers Ltd
Reception centre	No, but visitors are welcome. Tel: 049682-240
Established	c1810, rebuilt in 1960-3
Age when bottled	10 years
Strength	40%

TASTING NOTES

Nose	Smooth with subtle peaty traces. Dry.
Taste	Well matured, full but delicate flavour. Good lingering character.
Comments	An almost Highland-like malt created by W Delmé-Evans for drinking anytime. Always worth visiting the distillery by crossing the water when you are on Islay.

PERSONAL NOTES

Malt	**LEDAIG**
Distillery	Tobermory TOBERMORY, Mull, Argyll
Status	Tobermory Distillers Ltd
Reception centre	No
Established	1798

TASTING NOTES *(No age given, 40%)*

Nose	Fine, fruity nose.
Taste	Gentle flavour with a soft finish. A good, subtle malt.
Comments	Pre-dinner, from a distillery with a fascinating history. Available from the independent bottlers (see page 139).

PERSONAL NOTES

Tobermory distillery, Isle of Mull

Brand	**TALISKER**
Distillery	Talisker CARBOST, Isle of Skye
Status	United Distillers
Reception centre	Yes. Tel: 047842-203
Age when bottled	10 years
Established	1830-33
Strength	45.8%

TASTING NOTES

Nose	Heavy sweet and full aroma.
Taste	Unique full flavour which explodes on the palate, lingering with an element of sweetness.
Comments	Superb after-dinner malt from UDG's Classic Malt range. One of the best.

PERSONAL NOTES

HIGHLAND PARK ® ORKNEY

The Single Malt Scotch Whisky
From The Islands of Orkney

DISTILLED AND BOTTLED BY JAMES GRANT AND CO.
(HIGHLAND PARK DISTILLERY) LTD. KIRKWALL ORKNEY SCOTLAND

PRODUCT OF SCOTLAND

GDF001

Brand	**HIGHLAND PARK**
Distillery	Highland Park KIRKWALL, Orkney
Status	The Highland Distilleries Co plc
Reception centre	Yes. Tel: 0856-4619
Established	1795
Age when bottled	12 years
Strength	40%

TASTING NOTES

Nose	Full of character — pleasant, lingering and smokey.
Taste	Medium, well-balanced flavour finishing with a subtle dryness.
Comments	An excellent after-dinner dram from Scotland's most northerly distillery.

PERSONAL NOTES

Malt	**SCAPA**
Distillery	Scapa KIRKWALL, Orkney
Status	Allied Distillers Ltd
Reception centre	Tel: 0856-2071
Established	1885

TASTING NOTES (8 year old, 40%)

Nose	Delightful aromatic bouquet of peat and heather.
Taste	Medium-bodied with a malty, silk-like finish.
Comments	After-dinner, but only from the independent bottlers (see page 139). The Navy rescued Scapa from destruction by fire during the First World War!

PERSONAL NOTES

INDEPENDENT BOTTLERS

The following malts are not marketed as brands by
their respective distillers and are available from the
two main Scottish independent bottlers:

Gordon & MacPhail Ltd

50-60 South Street
ELGIN, Morayshire IV30 1JY
Tel: 0343-45111
Gordon and MacPhail usually give the year of
distillation instead of the age when bottled.
Strength is normally 40% alcohol by volume.

Cadenheads Whisky Shop

172 Canongate
EDINBURGH EH8 8BN
Tel: 031-556-5864 (retail & mixed cases)
Tel: 0586-52009 (wholesale)
William Cadenhead bottle malts at 46% alcohol by
volume and at a number of ages.

	G & M	Wm Cad
Aberfeldy	1970	
Ardmore		22 years old
Balmenach	1970/71	15, 18, 24 years old
Banff	1974	
Ben Nevis	1966	18, 22, 23 years old
Benriach	1969	21, 22 years old
Benrinnes	1968	22, 23, 26 years old
Benromach	1968	18 years old
Caol Ila	1972	
Caperdonich	1968/79	
Coleburn	1965/72	17 years old
Convalmore	1969	23, 28 years old
Craigellachie	1971	15, 16, 26 years old
Dailuaine	1971	22, 26 years old
Dallas Dhu	1970	26 years old
Glen Albyn	1963	20, 23 years old

Glencadam	1974	16, 21, 22, 25 years old
Glen Keith	1963/65	16, 17, 21 years old
Glenlochy	1974	20 years old
Glenlossie	1968/69	18 years old
Glen Mhor	8, 15 years old	21 years old
Glentauchers		20 years old
Glenugie	1966	20, 22 years old
Imperial	1970	
Inverleven		21 years old
Kinclaith	1966/67	20, 23 years old
Knockdhu	1974	
Ledaig	1973	
Lochside	1965/66	
Macduff	1963/75	21, 23 years old
Millburn	1966/71	13 years old
Mortlach	12, 21, 25 years old	17, 26 years old
Mosstowie	1970	
North Port	1970	
Old Pulteney	8, 15 years old; 1961	
Pittyvaich		12 years old
Port Ellen	1970	
Pulteney		17 years old
Royal Brackla	1970	
Scapa	8 years old; 1963	20, 23 years old
Spreyburn	1971	16, 21 years old
St Magdalene	1964	24 years old
Teaninich	1971	

THE KEEPERS OF THE QUAICH

The Keepers of the Quaich is a society formed by the major producers of Scotch whisky on the 16th October 1988. Its aims are to build on the value and prestige of Scotch whisky at home and abroad and to further interest in the lesser known aspects and attributes of the 'Spirit of Scotland'. The organisation includes leaders of society, industry and commerce from across the world, leaders of the Scotch whisky industry and noted Scotch whisky connoisseurs and characters. All have one fundamental link in common — a love of Scotland and Scotch whisky. The companies listed below represent almost the entire industry and so it is almost certain that the Keepers of the Quaich will become a permanent feature for the whisky trade worldwide. Under the patronage of (among others) His Grace, The Duke of Atholl, banquets are regularly held at Blair Castle in Perthshire to invest new members as Keepers and to promote not only Scotch but also Scotland. The seal of the society if therefore most appropriate — bestowed by the Lord Lyon, it proclaims UISGEBEATHA GU BRATH — Water of Life Forever.

FOUNDING PARTNERS
United Distillers
33 Ellersly Road
EDINBURGH EH12 6JW

United Distillers, the spirits company of Guinness plc, is the major producer of branded spirits in the UK with a portfolio of over 100 brands of Scotch whisky, gin, vodka and bourbon. UK sales are the responsibility of Perth-based Arthur Bell Distillers who were absorbed into the Guinness group prior to the takeover of The Distillers Company.

Allied Distillers Ltd
2 Glasgow Road
DUMBARTON G82 1ND

Incorporating George Ballantine & Son, William Teacher & Sons and Stewart & Son of Dundee this new company formed in January 1988 focuses the inter-related whisky interests of Hiram Walker-Allied Vintners, the wines and spirits arm of Allied-Lyons plc. Headquartered in Dumbarton where the parent company operates the largest grain whisky distillery in Scotland, the new company continues an association with the town first started in 1938 by Hiram Walker.

Justerini & Brooks Ltd
17 Cornwall Terrace
LONDON NW1 4QP

This company was founded in 1749 by Giacomo Justerini, an Italian cordial maker who came to London in pursuit of an Opera singer. He failed in his quest for the lady, but remained to form a commercial alliance with George Johnson and together they set themselves up as wine merchants. By 1760 the company had been granted the first of its eight successive Royal Warrants and in 1830 the company was bought by Alfred Brooks. A century later the house brand of Scotch — J&B Rare dominated the company's exports to the United States. After merging with Twiss Brownings and Hallowes to form United Wine Traders, the company bought Gilbeys in 1962 to form International Distillers and Vintners, now the drinks division of Grand Metropolitan.

**The Highland Distilleries Co plc &
Robertson & Baxter Ltd
106 West Nile Street
GLASGOW G1 2QY**

The Highland Distilleries Company was
incorporated in July 1887 as distillers of high
quality malt whisky for the blending trade having
secured the ownership of both Glenrothes and
Bunnahabhain distilleries. Having acquired
Glenglassaugh distillery in 1892 and Tamdhu in
1898, the company expanded its interests and
later formed a close association with whisky
brokers Robertson & Baxter Ltd. The malt
portfolio was enlarged with the addition of
Highland Park in Orkney in 1937 and its blended
whisky interests were also furthered with the
takeover of Matthew Gloag & Sons Ltd, the
Perth blenders of The Famous Grouse in 1970.

CORPORATE MEMBERS

**James Burrough Distillers plc
1780 London Road
GLASGOW G32 8XA**

**Campbell Distillers Ltd
West Byrehill
KILWINNING KA13 6LE**

**Findlater Mackie Todd & Co Ltd
Deerpark Road
Merton Abbey
LONDON SW19 3TU**

**J&G Grant
Glenfarclas Distillery
Marypark
BALLINDALLOCH
Banffshire AB3 9BD**

William Grant & Sons Ltd
Independence House
84 Lower Mortlake Road
RICHMOND
Surrey TW9 2HS

Invergordon Distillers Ltd
9-21 Salamander Place
EDINBURGH EH6 7JL

William Lawson Distillers Ltd
288 Main Street
COATBRIDGE ML5 3RH

Macallan Glenlivet plc
CRAIGELLACHIE
Banffshire AB3 9RX

Macdonald Martin Distillers plc
186 Commercial Street
Leith
EDINBURGH EH6 6NN

Morrison Bowmore Distillers Ltd
Springburn Bond
Carlisle Street
GLASGOW G21 1EQ

The North British Distillery Co Ltd
Wheatfield Road
EDINBURGH EH11 2PX

The Seagram Company Ltd
Seagram Distillers House
Dacre St
LONDON SW1 0DR

Whyte & Mackay Distillers Ltd
Dalmore House
296/298 St Vincent Street
GLASGOW G2 5RG

INDEX